Communication skills for engineers and scientists

Institution of Chemical Engineers

Published by
Institution of Chemical Engineers
Davis Building
165–189 Railway Terrace
Rugby
Warwickshire CV21 3HQ, UK

Telephone: 01788 578214
International: +44 1788 578214

Facsimile: 01788 560833
International: +44 1788 560833

ISBN 0 85295 354 2

First Edition 1990
Second Edition 1994
Reprinted 1995

Printed in the UK by Chameleon Press Ltd, 5–25 Burr Road,
Wandsworth, London SW18 4SG

Introduction

Good communicators are rare; most people have to work hard to ensure that the correct message is given to the right person at the right time, and that the message has been received and understood.

If communicators are made, not born, how can you join them? And why should you?

Well, your job will be easier if you are a good communicator, and your chances of promotion will be improved because you will be operating efficiently.

Information must be given to your customers, the people you work with, and those who work for you; and they are not all engineers or scientists. You may need to present a good case to the Managing Director, or the Chief Accountant. If you are appointed to lead a project team, you must be sure that everyone knows what is going on so that they can work efficiently. So, first of all, whether writing or speaking, *what are you trying to say*?

On the other hand, you may need to know how the workforce is taking a change in the organization. Not all messages are verbal; good communication involves listening, observing and reading too.

Whatever your objective, this booklet will help you to get the message across, and to receive the answers loud and clear. The booklet is in ten sections; each section tackles a particular aspect of communication skills.

Contents

" Good
communicators
are born, not made ...
... but study and
a little practice can
work wonders **"**

Anon

1. Basic rules and basic tools

Basic rules

1.　　Once you have identified your objective, suit your method to the job in hand — that is, use the most efficient way of (a) communicating the information you need to pass on, or (b) obtaining the information you need. For example:

• a simple question/ request	use the telephone
• a complicated problem/set of instructions	write it down and ask for for a written reply, if necessary
• a few people need to know	write a memo with 'Copies to' listed
• a team or section must be kept informed	hold regular briefing meetings, and issue notes on key points afterwards

2.　　Before you start, ask yourself the following questions.
(a)　　Getting the message across:
• who needs to know and when?
• what do they need to know?
• how should they receive the information and how often?
(b)　　Receiving the answer loud and clear:
• what is the purpose of the information you have received?
• why you? What are you expected to do next?
• how do you retain/retrieve the information when required?
• what else do you need to know/check before you can act?

3.   Always log your action, noting the time, who you spoke to, and what was agreed. Use your diary to keep these notes or, if you deal with many enquiries, keep a day book, with columns for date, time, message and action. If necessary, ask for written confirmation — for example, 'Would you mind dropping me a line confirming that price/delivery date please?'.

4.   Always be polite, considerate and diplomatic, irrespective of the seniority of your opposite number. Assume they are trying to be helpful until it becomes obvious that they are not. Even then *keep your cool*!

5.   Make sure that you have made your credentials/ needs clear before making a request, particularly if you want special treatment.

6.   Remember that shared goals may not lead to agreement on the means of achieving them.

7.   Be concise — time is money!

8.   Remember that many problems and misunderstandings first surface in general chat. Any responsible person must always be ready to talk, listen, observe and resolve, if necessary, or raise the problem in general terms at an appropriate moment.

9.   If in doubt, ask.

10.   If you don't know, say so. Fudging the answer is poor communication.

11.   Try and show the other person how answering your questions will help both of you. Then you'll get more cooperation.

Basic tools

Words are the basic tools of communication. Obvious, yes, but just how large is your vocabulary?

Some of us need no more than 600–800 words for getting through daily life, while an average, educated person may use a range of more than 5000 words as a matter of course. A demanding profession will require additional specialized terms, which must be used precisely in context.

As you move from speaking to writing, your vocabulary should increase, partly because the day-to-day shorthand of speech is no longer appropriate, and partly because you must introduce a greater variety of expression to avoid boring your reader. How many new words have you acquired lately? Do you look up a word if you have not met it before? Do you notice how good writers vary the length of their sentences, and their use of words?

Four types of publication can help you to improve the way you use words.

Dictionary

To use words correctly, you must appreciate their meanings, and know how to spell them. There are many standard works, such as the *Concise Oxford Dictionary*, but you may find a new-style volume, prepared by the University of Birmingham and published by Collins, more helpful. The *Collins Cobuild Essential English Dictionary* (edited by J.M. Sinclair) includes extended advice on how to use a word, and explains how its meaning can change according to the context. For example, the word 'back' enjoys 37 listed meanings before the editors move on to such expressions as 'back off', 'back out' and, for computer users, 'back up'.

Thesaurus

Constant repetition of a word, whether in a presentation or in a written report, can be both irritating and boring. Alternatives are presented in a thesaurus. The classic is by Roget (paperback edition by Penguin). The *New Collins Thesaurus* is a wordfinder in dictionary form which you may find easier to use. It contains

275,000 alternatives for 16,000 main entry words, demonstrating all too clearly why we need help when it comes to searching for another way of saying the same thing.

Grammar and style
Basic advice on the structure of sentences, punctuation, grammar and style can be found in such booklets as *Common Errors in English Language* by S.R. Golding (MacMillan Education) and *English Made Simple* by A. Waldhorn and A. Zeiger (W.H. Allen). Intended for those revising for school examinations in English, these little books will remind you of the rules you should have remembered! To raise your command of English to a higher plane, you should study *The Complete Plain Words* by Sir Ernest Gowers (Penguin) and H.W. Fowler's *Dictionary of Modern English Usage* (Oxford University Press).

Specific guides
Low-cost booklets on *Report Writing*, *Tips on Talking* and so on can be obtained from the British Association for Commercial and Industrial Education (BACIE).

Finally, the use of diagrams and illustrations has not been forgotten. These aids to communication are discussed in Section 6.

2. Listen, observe, read with profit

Listening and observing

Listening should be an active, not a passive state. A good listener will learn more than an uninterested or unsympathetic one, first by listening carefully to both the words and the tone of voice, and second by asking well-placed questions which indicate understanding and involvement. The task is made easier if the listener pays attention to the speaker's body language.

Unfortunately, many engineers and scientists simply do not notice body language; yet facial expressions, hand and foot movements and general body attitudes can tell you a lot.

As a good listener, you need to register interest or approval, but under certain circumstances you may want to indicate boredom, disbelief or even anger. How can you do this without actually speaking? When you are next bored (at a meeting or a lecture, perhaps) start noting how often you fidget, look at your watch, sigh heavily, gaze at the floor or out of the window or anywhere but at the speaker — all body language!

How can you improve your listening techniques? First of all, you must accept that you cannot possibly remember everything you hear, but you can learn to concentrate. If your mind wanders, or you become conscious that the chair is hard, it may tell you something about the speaker, but it could also mean that greater self-discipline is needed from you. Remember that a good listener is well on the way to becoming a good speaker.

Positive listening enables you to select those points you must remember. Ice-breaking or general pleasantries can be disregarded, but *look* interested! When a significant remark is made, the listener should show that this has been realized, perhaps by leaning forward slightly or smiling, to encourage the line of thought and to assist the memory. At the same time, keep track of the speaker's body language. Can you work out which are the weakest points in his argument from his behaviour alone?

In informal situations you cannot take notes, but you can jot down any interesting remarks, or leads, in your diary later. Take notes at formal lectures or meetings, but do not try to write down everything or you will miss the messages given in the speaker's body language. Note down key words or phrases. Good speakers will indicate by their tone which points are important. If notes or papers are available, it may be better to focus on what the speaker is emphasizing, and follow up by reading the notes or papers later. As many technical presentations are very detailed, the audience should be provided with prepared notes so that they can concentrate on the reasoning.

To help you to improve your ability to listen and observe constructively, try the following exercises:

• Check your recall level after listening to a news bulletin on the radio (do not take notes).

• Repeat the exercise, noting down key words and phrases; compare the quality of your recall.

• When you are watching a politician on TV, list the body movements which tell you he is trying to avoid answering the question. Or note the number and type of 'filling-in' phrases he uses to avoid the point of the question. Repeat the exercise for any spokesman attempting to explain an unfortunate decision or occurrence.

• What sort of messages can a listener send to a speaker by body language? List the movements, and their meanings.

• Attend a lecture with a friend, agreeing beforehand which one of you will take notes, and discuss the presentation afterwards. Who gained the most from the lecture, and why?

• When dealing with a customer, staff reporting to you, or someone trying to give you information, how do you decide when to intervene, and how do you know whether your contribution has been favourably/unfavourably received? If you do not know, start observing now — you are losing out.

Reading for work and pleasure

Professionals must be well informed and up to date in their specialization. They should also be well read in the general sense. The difficulty comes in finding the time for reading, and selecting the best reading material.

• First, look critically at the documents you receive at work, such as progress reports, safety reviews, technical proposals, magazines, books and learned society papers. Make a list of the important magazines you should read for your job; then weed it. How many are really vital? Do the same for other publications. Would a copy of the contents page suffice, with the ability to call for a journal or book if it looks promising?

• When you have compiled your essential reading list, stick to it, but update it every six months as your requirements may change.

• Set a definite time for technical reading — so many hours per week.

• Improve your reading rate, perhaps through selecting key sections of a paper or an article — for example, the summary, introduction, conclusion or the first sentence of each paragraph — and then checking your comprehension level as against the complete paper.

• Increase your reading rate (take a course).

• Check your retention level.

• Mark key sections or make your own one-line summary of essentials on the cover.

Reading for work
Begin by answering the following questions:

• How many commercially produced magazines do you read for technical information?

- Do you read articles or scan advertisements?

- How long do you devote to any one publication?

- Where do you do your work reading — on the train, in the lunch hour, at home?

- Have you time for reading at work?

- How much do you read, and should it be more or less in relation to its importance to your job?

- How quickly do you read, and could you improve your speed?

- How well do you retain what you read?

- Do you keep records or abstracts of important references?

- Do you use your free time for wider technical reading to do your job better?

- Rank the importance to your work of the technical literature you read.

Reading for pleasure
- How do you choose the newspaper you read?

- How many books and what types — for example, novels, biographies, travel — do you read in a year?

- List the books you read last year.

- How many of the plots can you summarize?

- How many new words did you absorb, and how many did you look up?

3. Telephone skills count

Telephones are quick and convenient to use. The problem is that they must be answered and, if there is no-one else about, you may have to deal with an enquiry or a complaint outside your own knowledge.

A good telephone manner is a great asset. You should cultivate a personal, friendly style. As someone once said, let the person receiving the call hear your smile. But remember, an over-long phone call can be counter-productive as it may stop the 'receiver' from attending to urgent business. As a rule of thumb, if your question or message is reasonably brief, use the phone. Complex matters which require detailed discussion merit a letter or a visit, and in every case, if things need to be made official, written confirmation is necessary. However, if the occasion demands it, continue the call until a satisfactory and clear understanding has been reached on both sides, particularly if you are dealing with a complaint.

Dos and don'ts

• Aways give your name and company name when making a call.

• State your business clearly — remember that the person at the other end is thinking of something else. People are rarely sitting waiting for you to ring.

• Take notes as you speak and listen.

• Make sure you know who you are speaking to and what their position is.

• Avoid discussion of confidential matters.

• Relax and use an interested tone of voice — the phone emphasizes tone and speech characteristics. If you speak quickly it will just be gabbling to the listener.

- Be reasonably brief without being curt.

- If you do not know the answer, say so, and offer help in finding it.

- Say you will ring back if you need time to think. Don't make hasty judgments.

- Do not allow a call to interrupt a meeting or interview unless it is vital.

- Make it clear that you are following the speaker's argument — they cannot see your face, so some verbal encouragement is needed.

- If you are faced with a complex message for a colleague, either say you will get them to ring back or suggest the caller should write a note.

- Never just say 'hello' when answering the phone; it is best to give your department and your name.

- Whatever you promise to do as a result of a call, do it quickly!

Dealing with long-winded callers
- Indicate politely that time presses.

- Tone down the subtle approach. For example, 'I must go, I am in the middle of ...'

- Insist on the need for written instructions/documentation before you can act.

- If all else fails, get yourself cut off!

Dealing with irate callers
Irate callers are often incoherent; rage and frustration seem to render them incapable of even telling you their names, let alone the reason for their call.

- Try to get the caller to tell you the story from the beginning — say, 'I will try to help you but I do not have the whole story, please tell me'.

- Be helpful and calm.

- Do not offer to transfer them until you are sure you are putting them on to the right person — the wrong one will enrage them further!

- Get them to give you their name, address and phone number, and the cause of their complaint/problem. Promise to ring back when you have found out what is wrong, or get the right person to do this. *Then do it!* Don't think that getting them to put the phone down lets you off the hook.

Dealing with telephone enquiries
Remember that an enquiry could turn into an order so deal with the caller efficiently and courteously. Get down:
- name of enquirer;
- position;
- company address and telephone number, plus fax if they have it;
- company business;
- nature of enquiry;
- time you took the enquiry and the date.

Then:
- Record what you have done — for example, 'I will get X, the engineer in charge, to ring you back today' (check with the caller if they will be available).

- Make copies for those involved in the response, and keep a copy for yourself.

- If need be, check that action has been taken.

Your company may have a telephone enquiry system. If not, you could suggest it is worth having both a system and a follow-up procedure.

Finally, you may speak to unsolicited callers who ask for information but whose purpose is not clearly stated. They may be 'researchers' compiling mailing lists, telephone salespersons, or whatever. And harassed switchboard operators put them through because it is not obvious what they want.

If it is not clear why they are calling, check particularly:

- what information is needed and why they want it;
- who is speaking and what their company's business is.

Make it clear that they should make an appointment to see the appropriate person, or ask them to put their request in writing to the Company Secretary. Do not agree to see them yourself, or answer a few questions — you could waste hours!

4. Writing the message down

Whether you are writing a letter, instructions, an article or a report to a client, first decide what you want to say.

Then decide which form you will use — for instance, letter or memo. What does the recipient need to know if he is to understand the message?

Next, using key words, make a brief outline of the document.

Letter outline
1.　　State the purpose of your letter clearly.
2.　　Highlight particular points which are essential to your argument/sales pitch/request or whatever.
3.　　Ask for any further information you need.
4.　　Set out your conclusion — you might say you need information by a certain date.
5.　　Add the appropriate signing off phrases.

Report outline
1.　　Title.
2.　　Background.
3.　　Objectives.
4.　　Techniques used.
5.　　Results.
6.　　Benefits or conclusions.
7.　　Further information, references, acknowledgements, etc.

General rules
• Whatever you are writing, stick to the point. Read back what you have written — does it say what you mean? If you are unsure, get colleagues to read the document through and get them to tell you what they think you are saying.

• Cut out superfluous material.

- Check for repetition of words and phrases — find synonyms in the thesaurus.

- Check grammar. For example, if the subject is singular, the verb should take the singular form; weed out split infinitives; use the active rather than the passive voice; and so on.

- Make sure you have got your facts right.

- Try to ensure that you cannot be misconstrued if the document deals with a tricky subject. Put yourself in the position of the reader; reread what you have written, and if you feel threatened or insulted, the letter is over the top. Tone it down (equally it could be an instruction or a memo).

- Don't try to score off people.

- Remember that written material of all kinds is on the record.

- Keep copies, and get yourself a good filing system so that you can always retrieve information when it is needed.

- Keep confidentiality in mind according to the audience you are writing for.

- Remember that for the people who do not know you personally, what you write is you!

Notes, memos and letters: dos and don'ts

- Check the typing and the spelling before you send documents out.

- Use them to confirm arrangements made on the telephone — bookings, train times, meeting details and so on.

- If you need to go into details, put them on a separate sheet as an attachment.

- Make sure you send copies to the people who need to know (attach a list of 'Copies to').

- Use a contrasting colour for added impact if you are using handwriting.

- Don't use handwritten notes if your handwriting is poor.

Technical papers and reports: dos and don'ts

- An inadequate report can ruin good technical performance. It is in your interest to work hard on your report.

- Be sure to provide a concise abstract which states the reason for the work, name of the client, main results and conclusions. This may be all the Managing Director or Chief Engineer reads; others will do the detailed assessment.

- Keep jargon to a minimum.

- Vary sentence length. If all sentences are the same length, the result is boring, and a report that is all short sentences has an aggressive tone. A series of long sentences is even worse!

- Plan the report structure carefully.

- Conclusions should be clear and specific.

- Give proper acknowledgements and provide a bibliography with papers.

- Finally, before you write that paper, make sure it is necessary (don't write just to improve your publication average).

All these rules apply to technical proposals and case justifications. Above everything, be concise and try to put yourself in the place of the client or manager and then answer 'their' questions. Clients need to know what is in the proposal for them and their company. Make it clear!

Finally, practice. People who write for a living know that there is no ideal way to say anything. Even great authors are constantly refining their style.

To help you, attempt the following exercises, and then read your efforts critically. Try again!

- You are off on two weeks' holiday. Prepare notes for the person who is to look after your post and progress your work while you are away. Watch that you give clear instructions but do not over-do it — you could alienate your colleague.

- Draft a letter to schools offering help with the introduction of technology into the classroom and outline a visit programme to your place of work.

- A friend asks you for help in finding a job. Draft a sympathetic but negative reply which will not offend.

- Imagine you are secretary of the company social club and the club is running a big charity function. Draft a letter to a local personality (or a national one) asking for their help but making it clear that you are not offering a fee. Assume you were successful, and write a letter of thanks.

- Take your latest report and see if you can cover the same ground using half the number of words.

- Prepare an outline for a report describing the most complex technical aspects of your work. Then prepare a summary for the Managing Director.

- Take reports produced by your organization and write abstracts of no more than 500 words.

- Assess notes and business letters you have received and note whether they offer you all the information you needed, or whether they were too long. Try rewriting the least satisfactory — but discreetly ... your actions might be misinterpreted.

5. Public speaking, or talking tells

Whether you are holding a conversation or addressing a large meeting, you need to remember that your listeners are not just taking in the words. They are also registering your tone of voice, your body language, and your general manner and appearance. In fact, if your non-verbal communication is odd or too violent they may not hear what you say. Instead, they could be wondering why you cannot stand still.

All good public speakers practise. They prepare their presentation and its delivery with equal thoroughness. But before getting down to public speaking, here are a few pointers on conversation and dealing with visitors.

Conversations and visits

Many important orders arise from good personal contacts. You need to get on to a relaxed and friendly footing so that your opposite number feels comfortable with you. Then they can tell you about their problems, which could make all the difference when it comes to progressing work. For example, if you know that the department is being reorganized/computerized, you can include some leeway in your timetable in case of problems. And if you smooth the way for them this time, they could help you in the future when you experience difficulties.

You may be visiting another company, they may be visting you, or you could be invited to a social event. In each case the same rules apply:

- Eye contact is important — when you greet a visitor, look at them, smile and sound pleased to see them.

- Small talk is never a waste of time; it leads to bigger things. Half the battle is getting started. Prepare a few general enquiries about the journey, the weather, etc. If your memory is bad, keep notes on people you deal with regularly so that you can ask about their promotion/family/new car ... all ice-breakers.

- Know when to move the conversation on. Body language should tell you — your guest's if not your own!

- Listen carefully throughout the day; the most important information may be given in the car park as you see the visitor off or you leave.

- If the visit is over-running or going badly, have a few polite disengagement strategies ready but use them subtly to avoid offence.

- Let your guest/host finish speaking, don't cut in in your eagerness to make your point.

- Time is money, so try to keep to the point once the real discussion starts.

- If you are going to deliver a bombshell, do it tactfully.

- There is nothing wrong with a false start, people do it all the time. But work hard to recover the position.

- Don't laugh too much at your own jokes — they may not be funny — but ensure that the hearer knows it is a joke. Overseas visitors in particular may need help.

- If your company receives foreign visitors regularly, check on their ideas of politeness. For example, Japanese will bring gifts but it is not polite to open the package until the visitors have gone. If they are to be given a present, wrap it for this reason. Thanks and enthusiasm for the gift should be shown.

- Finally, if you are relaxed, friendly and enthusiastic, your visitors will be too.

Public speaking

Your public could consist of two or three colleagues, a group of clients, or the audience at a major technical conference. However large or small the numbers, you need to prepare your

presentation carefully — the words, the visuals and the timing.
First, what is the objective of your talk?

The words
- Prepare the structure of the talk carefully and logically.

- Write out the presentation initially, and read out each section.
Cut out anything you cannot say easily, or reword it so that
you have natural breathing spaces (at the end of phrases
or sentences).

- Then prepare cue cards which give the key words and
phrases — never read anything out word for word.

- List the visuals to be used wth each card — put them in a
different colour or give them a column on their own so that you
do not overlook or muddle them.

- After the initial greeting (for example, 'Good morning,
ladies and gentlemen'), tell the audience what you are
about to tell them, then tell them, and at the end tell them
what you have told them. It will help them to remember
your contribution.

- Be yourself — don't try to overwrite. Use words you are
comfortable with.

- Humour is good, but be careful with set jokes. It takes years to
develop a comedian's sense of timing.

- Keep to the time allowed. If it's up to you, keep it short.

- Stick to essentials — don't try to show how much you know or
have done.

- Leave time for discussion. Plant a question or two in the
audience's mind.

- Prepare a summary of the main points of your talk, if
appropriate, ready to hand out afterwards.

Timing and delivery

• Speak up and speak clearly. Don't gabble or pause distractedly (the audience will think you have forgotten what you were saying).

• Allow short pauses at key points so that the message can sink in.

• Vary your delivery — that is, change your speed slightly and your pitch.

• Do not fiddle with your keys, loose change, or the desk furniture. It is very distracting.

• Use your hands to emphasize points naturally.

• Look at the audience. Above all do not face the screen behind you and talk to it!

• Don't rush about too much. Pacing up and down before the audience will give them all 'tennis match' neck.

• Keep an eye on the audience's body language.

• Know when to stop.

It is a good idea to practise inflexions and speed changes when you are preparing the words. Timing yourself at this stage will help you to tailor your presentation to the time allowed, as well as making sure that you get the message across.

Visuals are covered in Section 6.

6. Visual aids

One picture is worth a thousand words, Confucius said. But it all depends on the picture, and on the type of talk you are preparing, or the article you are writing.

You could use actual hardware, films, video, slides, overhead projection (OHP), a flip-chart or a blackboard to illustrate your point. For technical talks in general, keep your aids simple. The more complex your battery of projectors the more things can go wrong!

This section deals with the items you are most likely to be able to prepare at work — slides and diagrams. The general rules are the same for illustrating an article as for a talk.

Dos and don'ts

• Never overdo the visual aids. A slide saying 'Hello, I'm John of Company X' is hardly necessary.

• Keep the visuals simple so that the information they contain can be absorbed.

• Use colour on your slides but avoid orange and yellow which do not show up very well when projected. For text only, white or yellow out of blue or black is pleasant to look at and easy to read.

• Try to limit words per slide to a maximum of 10. Use a reasonable size, blocky typeface which will enlarge well. Do not use ordinary typing.

• Go for clear, bold concepts in visuals. They will project better and are easier to take in.

• Get your OHPs done in the same way and limit the number of additions you make during the talk — the audience will be fascinated by your shaking hand!

• Use colour photographs whenever possible, but check that they are not too cluttered and that they do not contain obvious safety hazards — you will get questions on the hazards and not the work if you are not careful.

• Ensure that your company logo is on each slide — discreetly and always in a standard place (for example, bottom left-hand corner).

• Edit your slides as carefully as your talk — if a slide does not advance your message, cut it out. If you want to use a slide twice, duplicate it.

Tips on the dark
• Avoid too much dark; some people seem to go to sleep the moment the lights go out! It could be something to do with TV!

• Switch off the projector when it is not being used.

• Use your illustrations in batches; don't spend half your time turning lights on and off.

Diagrams
Avoid the temptation to try and use the diagram prepared for a technical report in your talk. It will undoubtedly be too detailed, like the examples shown on pages 23 and 24.

If you have a printing department or a photography section in your company, check the facilities they offer. There are various methods of making crisp, colourful overheads, slides, computer-generated colour reproductions and so on, using many different typefaces, to help you to put the message across.

One word of warning. Give these services reasonable notice if you want their help. Do not breeze in and ask for 20 slides by midday as a matter of course. They need time to produce good work too!

Original
diagram

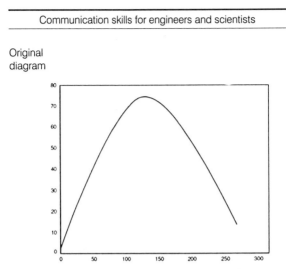

Fig 4 Example of savings in fuel costs when injecting fuel into a blast furnace

Visual
for talk

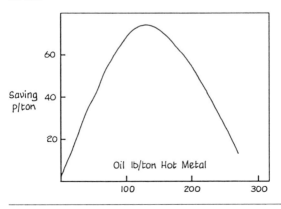

Original
diagram

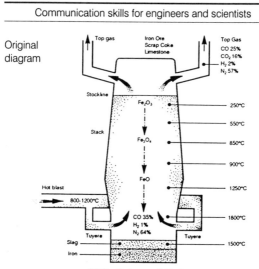

FIG 1 Principle of operation of a blast furnace

Visual
for talk

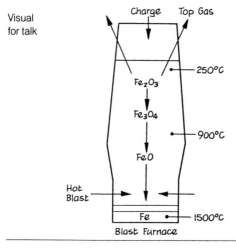

7. Meetings

You will probably have to attend briefing meetings and committees of some kind during your career; very few professionals manage to avoid such things.

Badly run, committee meetings can be costly, time-consuming and very boring. With a good Chairman, an efficient Secretary and a carefully selected group of members, committees can bring the benefits of wide experience, a range of technical and professional expertise and the democratic process to effective decision-making.

Briefing meetings are essentially a method of exchanging information with the work team. Don't forget you want to know why they can't do what is being asked, what the snags are, etc. But the meetings can also be used to check how well the team understands management decisions and overall company goals.

Committees

Rules for Chairmen
- Once you have been made Chairman, ensure that everyone knows why they have been invited to attend the meeting. If you can influence numbers, keep the committee small.

- Prepare the agenda well in advance. Check the minutes of the last meeting. Keep your objectives in mind.

- If you can, keep notes and write the minutes yourself. It may save much time and effort.

- Be impartial, avoid favouritism and stop time-wasters or self-publicists firmly.

- Do not dominate the proceedings; a well-timed intervention is more effective.

- Be courteous to all, and ensure that everyone follows your lead.

• Summarize and confirm important decisions and allocate responsibilities clearly for each item on the agenda before tackling the next.

• Conclude the meeting by setting the date for the next meeting. It gives all present the opportunity to check their diaries.

Rules for committee members

• Study the paperwork before the meeting, do your homework thoroughly and check that you have fulfilled your allocated responsibilities.

• Follow the Chairman's lead.

• Address all remarks to the Chair.

• Express yourself clearly and concisely; keep to the point.

• Listen carefully to other speakers, and observe their body language.

• Accept your fair share of tasks.

• Expect to work as a team, and be ready to compromise for the common good.

• Cooperate with the Secretary.

Tasks for Secretaries

• Consult the Chairman on the agenda well before the meeting. If there must be a change in arrangements, let everyone know as soon as possible. Phone first and confirm in writing.

• Ensure that the agenda and any other papers are distributed to all in good time.

• Traditionally the Secretary remains silent at the meeting, other than helping on matters of fact and the minutes. (Nowadays the Secretary may also be a well-informed participant.) Procedure is also your responsibility so be sure you know the rules, and remind the Chairman politely if he strays.

• Don't try to record everything for the minutes. Write key words and phrases down. The Chairman's summaries of decisions and responsibilities are vital.

• Concentrate on recording ideas and discussion (not people).

• If you are not clear, ask for a point to be repeated or clarified.

• Resist pressure to 'improve' the minutes, but try to present contributions fairly and objectively (leave out the heated argument touches).

• Demonstrate your infinite patience and tact by reconciling the competing and inconsistent demands of the committee members!

Working parties or subcommittees
If the main committee is too big, setting up working parties can be helpful if:
• you have a real job to be done quickly and efficiently;
• the job demands a high level of expertise and involvement;
• painful decisions must be faced;
• confidentiality is essential.

Briefing meetings
Briefing meetings can be used at many levels: Managing Director to his departmental managers; managers to their department or section heads; section heads or project leaders to their team. They should be informal but, if you are doing the briefing, you should structure your remarks.

The briefing explains management or project decisions to the people who must apply them and make them work. You can cover the ground if you concentrate on the five Ps:
• policy;
• progress;
• problems;
• people;
• points for action.

Allow time for reaction; new problems and misunderstandings can surface. As the responsible person you must observe and listen, as well as talk, and you must be ready to resolve or explain, if possible. If not, you must be prepared to take the matter up with your manager. Properly used, the briefing can help to weld the team together, giving members a sense of the importance of their contributions and a feeling that they count.

Once you have set up, say, monthly briefings, you should be able to ensure that they last about half an hour (one hour as the maximum) without seeming to curtail the exchange you are aiming for. The time should only be extended if it's obvious that there is an important misunderstanding which affects everyone. One person with a probem should be invited to tell you about it in further detail after the meeting ... 'hang on for a moment X and we'll go through that again just to make sure I have got it right'. That way the rest of the team can get on with the job, and you can decide quietly if it is a genuine problem or pure cussedness!

8. Handling conflict

You must get on with people at work but you don't have to like them! In other words, keep emotion out of your work, if you can.

The essence is not to take things personally; an argument is not an attack on *you*, and *your* disagreements with your colleagues should not be on a personal basis either. Remind yourself you are debating a point — of policy, technical feasibility, economic reality. Whether X admires your bright blue eyes or not is irrelevant!

Most conflicts appear to stem from misunderstandings, and it is easy to list a host of reasons. For example:

- not listening properly;
- careless reading of instructions;
- poor instructions, with the most important detail left out, like the famous Mrs Beeton recipe for jugged hare which begins 'First catch your hare'. Not as obvious as it seems!
- lack of attention to the matter in hand by all concerned;
- arguments about who should do the job;
- making assumptions ('I thought you would do that') and not checking.

Add some more reasons for conflict from your own experience, and also note the remedy.

In spite of every precaution, problems will still arise. The potential for friction exists even in the best-run companies. For example:

- in technical situations, assumptions must be made, and colleagues can differ over which assumptions can be justified;
- deadline pressures can upset some people, while others respond well, leading to hold-ups, recriminations, and so on;
- compromise between safety and economic considerations can lead to serious differences on moral issues, and on costs;
- collaborators may turn into rivals if promotion beckons;
- competition may make the world go round but it also promotes conflict.

Bearing such factors in mind, you will have to accept that conflict is inevitable. You need to be alert, ready to note the unexpected reaction and to admit that your argument has weak spots. A good boss can always pick on the weak spot; if you find that the flaw in your plan had never occurred to you, work out why not. Is it a case of 'not one part of my golden plan should be changed'? Could your attitude be possessive, and therefore emotional?

Before starting to think of remedies, it is as well to ask yourself if the company style is the one likely to suit you and enable you to give of your best. If you cannot handle competitive selling, say, better to find another niche.

Dos and don'ts

Assuming you are in the right job, the following dos and don'ts should help you.

• Ensure that a simple misunderstanding is not the cause of the trouble.

• Face up to a problem positively.

• Stay calm and be polite.

• State your case quietly and do not repeat yourself, then shut up!

• Listen attentively to the reply or comment — there may be a face-saving formula for you both which leads to agreement.

• No-one is always right — should you give way?

• If debate is justified, keep cool and review the pros and cons objectively to help isolate the real problem.

• Remember that you have to face your 'opponent' tomorrow, next week, and while you both work for the same company, so try to keep a friendly tone and a reasonable manner.

• Do not look for trouble; a few simple checks might enable you to put the matter right quietly and efficiently.

• If things look bad, why not suggest a cooling-off period — 'shall we sleep on it, and tackle the problem when we have had time to check on ...?'

• Make sure you know what company policy is before you start banging your head against it.

• Be prepared to agree to differ and accept that seniority may decide on the final solution.

• Remember that your 'opponent' may not have the authority to change the party line. An adjournment may give the chance to consult the boss.

• Do not provoke; your objective should be to get the best deal worked out.

• Leave the 'opposition' an acceptable escape route, and don't rub your 'win' in.

• Give way gracefully yourself when the argument goes against you.

• Ensure you survive to fight another day — you can only resign once!

Before you embark on an argument, ask yourself 'Where is my sticking point?'. If the matter will not affect your real goal or target, make what is a minor concession — it costs you little and you can reserve your energies for the big job.

If the contents of this section have fired your interest, there is a host of books on human psychology, motivation and conflict, starting with the populist *People Watching* by Desmond Morris. Add some of them to your reading list.

9. Job applications and CVs

Whether you are looking for your first job or trying to improve your career prospects, can you do anything to enhance your chances in the current job market? The answer is 'Yes'.

Your job-hunting could begin by:

- studying vacancies advertised in the press;
- making a list of companies you would like to work for.

Alternatively, you could contact selection consultants and agencies. The very fortunate might obtain a personal recommendation or be approached by a headhunter.

In times when jobs are hard to come by, advertised vacancies attract hundreds of replies. A campaign writing to companies you'd like to work for, but who are not advertising, can be more rewarding; your details will be on file when a vacancy does come up.

Assuming that you must make contact yourself, try to be both systematic and realistic about your approach.

First, what sort of job do you hope to get? What are the characteristics which you think the holder of that job should possess? Do these characteristics match your own? In other words, are you aiming for a job which suits your qualifications and your temperament? Be realistic about yourself, and then play to your strengths. Make a list of your strengths.

Do your homework before you tackle the actual application. Study the companies — look them up in *Kompass*, *Key British Enterprises* and other reference books. They are probably available in your local library. Note any mention of the companies in the business pages of the quality newspapers and specialist technical press. A day in the reference section of your local library will not be wasted.

If you are answering a job advert, study it in relation to what you have learned about both the company and yourself. (This is equally appropriate if you are just writing in hope).

Have you uncovered any clues which will help you in the preparation of your CV, and the covering letter you need to write?

If you have read and acted on the other advice in this booklet, you should be able to write a clear, confident and well-expressed letter, and if you need to telephone, your manner will be friendly and pleasant. However, a few extra tips may help to make your covering letter work for you.

The covering letter

Your covering letter should be polite and reasonably short. Someone may have to sort through scores or even hundreds of applications.

The letter should:

• state clearly the reason for writing. Either use the exact job description (copied from the advertisement) and say where and when you saw it — 'the *Times* on Thursday Xth of Month' or indicate you are writing to ask if there are any vacancies in the company for young graduates (specify);

• highlight your major strengths in relation to the job;

• add a short sentence or two about your interest in or suitability for the job;

• make it clear that you have enclosed a CV, and that you hope to hear from the company shortly.

Try to give a little individuality to your letter. For example, a mature woman applied for a job handling VAT in a company accounts office, even though the advertisement specified an age range of 28–35. The applicant wrote, 'I am 35 plus VAT, ie 41'. This appropriate touch of humour got her the job.

The point is that the humour was appropriate. If it is not, then do not attempt it!

If your handwriting is bad, type the letter, or get it typed. Check the spelling — many personnel departments put misspelt letters on the reject pile straight away. Use good writing paper — ruled paper from a scribbling pad makes it clear that you have made no effort at all.

Remember the letter is all the company has to go on in the first instance. *It is you!*

Your CV

Although the facts about you are constant, you may need to alter the emphasis you give to them, depending on the job you are applying for. If you have studied yourself and the company objectively, you will realize what adjustments you need to make. Just as each covering letter will be different, so your CV should be addressed to the specific job. But the basic rules are the same.

Get your CV typed and set out clearly. Try to limit the number of pages to a maximum of three, and staple or clip them together. The interviewing panel/person may have to read 20 CVs; make yours the easiest to read and handle. Type on one side of the paper only. Stick to the facts and give dates for each job. For example, 1992–1993 looks fishy — are you talking about two full years or three months? Better to put January 1992–November 1993. If it was only three months, put it another way — 'Temporary job with X, December 1992–March 1993, assisting contracts manager with tender details'.

Outline for your CV
1. Name.
2. Address.
3. Telephone numbers — home and work.
4. Date of birth.
5. Education — put your degrees first, and just your highest qualifications at school. As a subsection you can list other qualifications — for example, Diploma in Industrial Psychology — but do not list every short course you have ever attended.
6. Career details — begin with your present job, outline responsibilities, list any achievements you can claim as your own. Take care you can substantiate your claim; you could be closely questioned on your 'invention'. Add any relevant company details.
7. Personal details — such as status (married/single, children) and interests (keep it short and be specific — not 'sport' but 'badminton and rugby league'.

Remember that the interviewers may have to read all this material after they have finished their usual work. Make sure they don't give up halfway through. Keep your application short, neat and easy to handle.

Of course, all this effort may simply bring forth an application form. Keep a copy of your letter and the CV as sent to each company, and use the same information so that there are no discrepancies. It saves time too!

Fill in the application form either in neat handwriting or type it. Do not use capital letters throughout; they are difficult to read and you always run out of space, making the last line impossible to decipher. Return the form with another covering letter reiterating (in different words) your interest/suitability for the job. If there is a named person on the advertisement or covering note with the form, write to them 'Dear Mr Blank' and sign yourself 'Yours sincerely'. Use 'Yours faithfully' if you have to write 'Dear Sir/Madam'. Keep copies of these items too.

Finally, be patient. If you do not hear for some time, you could phone the personnel department and ask if there is any news of your application. Be prepared, not only with the facts and figures — for example, date of the job advertisement and when you last wrote — but also for possible disappointment. In such cases, be polite and friendly, and start again.

Section 10 gives advice on how to approach a job interview.

10. Interviews

The day before

Read through this booklet and note the advice which will help you to present yourself clearly as an efficient, pleasant professional.

Go through all the correspondence with the company, study your copy of the job application and the material you collected on the company's operations. Prepare your questions. Consider your appearance. Again the watchword is professional — clean, tidy and well turned out. Your shoes may be old but they should be clean!

On the day

Arrive about 15–20 minutes before the stated time, to give you chance to use the cloakroom. If you have a heavy overcoat or an overnight bag, ask if you can leave such items somewhere safe. When you are met by the personnel officer/secretary, get the name of the principal interviewer and his position in the company. If you are offered coffee while you wait, make sure you put your briefcase down before taking the cup. Don't end up juggling your possessions plus the cup. Remember that the people you meet before you go into the interview may well be asked for their opinion after you have gone, so be polite and pleasant to all. And the same stricture applies to any young engineer who is asked to show you round the plant, laboratory or even the office; his opinion will probably also be canvassed. When you go into the interview room, keep calm and don't rush. Smile, greet the interviewer/panel, say 'Good morning', and shake hands if this is expected. Sit when invited, sit still and look alert. Do not smoke unless you are told you may do so. Nowadays many people abhor smoking in the office and it may be more sensible to decline anyway.

The interview

Listen carefully to the opening remarks, make eye contact, and study the body language. When answering questions keep to the point but avoid abrupt, monosyllabic replies like 'Yes' and 'No'. Concentrate on your strengths when the opportunity occurs. Be positive, optimistic and friendly in your replies and avoid any suggestion of inflexibility. Ask for clarification if in doubt. If the interviewer just says 'Tell me about yourself', say 'In relation to this job I believe I have the following strengths ... ' This may lead them to invite you to describe your personality, or your interests. Do this briefly but always bearing in mind how you wish to present yourself. Use humour if you feel it is appropriate, but beware — *they* may not have a sense of humour!

Remember that the interview is your opportunity to show yourself at your best (and that does not mean showing off). And it is also the time when you can learn a lot about the organization you hope to join. When you can, ask the questions you have prepared on company organization/training/experience in other departments or other matters. Do your bit towards keeping the dialogue going.

If you find the interviewer is aggressive, remember Section 8 on Handling Conflict. Keep cool, maintain your principal points but concede gracefully where you can. Some interviewers try the 'psychological testing' technique. If they push you, try turning the question back — 'Could you explain why this factor/point/procedure is so particularly important, please?'.

Silence may be another ploy, in which case, ask an appropriate question from the list you have prepared. If you are the last candidate in a full day, they may be very grateful as the silence could just be interview fatigue.

Some final thoughts

Most interviews come down to the question, 'Will this person fit in with our organization and get on with the people who already work here?' and this is where your research into the company could help you. For that type of business, what sort of person would be best? When you have worked that out, you can at least highlight those strengths you have which would help you to fit in, and at the interview you can try to show this aspect of your character.

Your education, previous experience, etc, will have been studied and will have influenced your position on the short list. These factors are important and you may be asked to enlarge on various aspects but friendliness, adaptability, a generous outlook, co-operativeness and other such character attributes will be equally important. Cool judgement, firmness under pressure and skill in handling tricky situations may also be required. It is the factors which cannot be quantified which will influence the decision between equally well qualified candidates. If you are a good communicator, your chances are improved.